A Taste of Wordsworth

by

Margaret E. Bailey

Illustrated by S. Baskerville-Muscutt

The Dalesman Publishing Company Ltd.,
Clapham, Lancaster, LA2 8EB.
First published 1987
© Text, Margaret E. Bailey 1987

ISBN: 0 85206 903 0

Printed by Fretwell & Cox Limited.
Goulbourne Street, Keighley, West Yorkshire, BD21 1PZ.

Contents

Acknowledgements

The author would like to thank Pat, Lois, Lesley, Julia and Nigel for their critical appraisals of her baking efforts in testing some of the recipes; Kendal Library for obtaining out of print recipe books, the Curator of Dove Cottage Museum for help in identifying Sara's Gate and Steven Baskerville-Muscutt for his beautiful illustrations.

Steven Baskerville-Muscutt:

After qualifying as an architectural technician, he studied art at Nuneaton College of Art and is now a member of the Lakes Artists Society. He specialises in pen and ink drawings and works from his Ambleside gallery.

Useful Facts and Figures

Oven Temperatures:
The Table below gives recommended equivalents:

	C°	F°	Gas Mark
Very cool	110	225	¼
	120	250	½
Cool or slow	140	275	1
	150	300	2
Warm	160	325	3
Moderate	180	350	4
Moderately hot	190	375	5
Fairly hot	200	400	6
Hot	220	425	7
Very hot	230	450	8
	240	475	9

Measurements
All measurements are given in Metric, Imperial and American. Here is a guide:

Metric	Imperial	American
5 ml spoon	1 teaspoon	1 teaspoon
15 ml spoon	1 tablespoon	1 tablespoon
	2 tablespoons	3 tablespoons
	3½ tablespoons	4 tablespoons
	4 tablespoons	5 tablespoons

Spoon measures are level unless indicated otherwise.

Solid Measures

450 g butter	1 lb	2 cups/4 sticks
450 g flour	1 lb	4 cups
450 g granulated or caster sugar	1 lb	2 cups
450 g icing sugar	1 lb	3 cups

Liquid Measures

150 ml	¼ pint	⅔ cup
300 ml	½ pint	1¼ cups
450 ml	¾ pint	2 cups
600 ml	1 pint (20 fl oz)	2½ cups (16 fl oz)
900 ml	1½ pints	3¾ cups
1 litre	1¾ pints	5 cups (2½ pints)

NOTE: When making any of the recipes in this book, only follow one set of measures as they are not interchangeable.

Introduction

To many people, the name Wordsworth brings only the poet William to mind. But Dorothy, his younger sister, also emerged as a writer — not of poetry but of letters and journals. Her Grasmere Journals written between 1800 and 1803 provide a detailed picture of life at Dove Cottage. From these, and her letters, it has been possible to see what kind of things were eaten in the Wordsworth household even though she rarely went into much detail or gave recipes. Often she merely wrote, "I baked pies, and bread . . .", but there are many references to food which have been included in this book together with a recipe for the reader to try.

Dorothy was born in Cockermouth in Cumbria in 1771 but was still a small child when both her parents died. She was separated from her four brothers and sent to live with relatives at Halifax in Yorkshire. Later she lived with her grandparents in Penrith, but she always missed her brothers John, Christopher, Richard and William. The early death of their parents had left them in reduced financial circumstances and they were dependent on their relatives for their education and accommodation.

Having no family home where they could all be together, Dorothy longed for one of her own and dreamed of setting up home with William, with whom she had a particular affinity. Eventually her dream came true and she and William went to live in Dorset in 1795. Later they moved to Alfoxden near Nether Stowey to be nearer their friend Samuel Taylor Coleridge. It was there that Dorothy began her first Journal on 20th January 1798.

In the last few days of December 1799 Dorothy and William moved into a cottage on the main road from Ambleside outside Grasmere village. It was one of a group known simply as Town End, and had at some time earlier been a public house known as the 'Dove and Olive Branch' from whence its name of Dove Cottage, as it is now known, came. The rent was £5 per annum. It was there, a few months later, that she began her now famous Grasmere Journals. Her brothers John and William had "set off into Yorkshire after dinner at ½ past 2 o'clock, cold pork in their pockets. I left them at the turning of the Low-wood bay under the trees. My heart was so full that I could hardly speak to W. when I gave him a farewell kiss. I sate a long time upon a stone at the margin of the lake, and after a flood of tears my heart was easier . . . Came home by Clappersgate. Sate down very often, though it was cold. I resolved to write a journal of the time till W. and J. return, and I set about keeping my resolve because I will not quarrel with myself, and because I shall give Wm pleasure by it when he comes home again . . ." The date was Wednesday, May 14th, 1800.

The Wordsworths' lifestyle has sometimes been described as

frugal, even by Dorothy herself, and some believe they lived on a diet of bread, porridge, broth and springwater. Such a description is perhaps unfair and inaccurate. That they lived economically would be a more realistic description.

But if the fare in the Wordsworth household was simple, there was probably a good reason for it. When they first came to live at Grasmere, they had recently returned from Germany where they were so poor that at one town they were taken as vagrants. Dorothy was detained in the tower at the gates of the town until William could prove their identity.

Although a large debt was owed to their father's estate, it was many years before the Wordsworth children managed to recover their inheritance. Thus, in setting up home together, Dorothy and William had to manage on Dorothy's £100 legacy from her Uncle Crackanthorpe's will and on William's legacy from Raisley Calvert.

Raisley was the younger brother of William Calvert, his old school friend from Hawkshead. The brothers had inherited a sizeable fortune on their father's death. Well aware of William's financial problems and of his efforts to establish himself as a poet, Raisley offered to share his income with him and leave him a large enough legacy to enable him to live without having to follow a profession. William agreed to become his companion on a journey to Portugal in 1794. They only got as far as Penrith when they had to return because of Raisley's failing health. William remained at the Calvert house in Keswick to nurse his friend who eventually died in January 1795. Raisley left him a legacy of £900.

As housekeeper Dorothy was very much aware of their limited resources. Being a single woman, she was basically dependent on her brothers for money, and she had to ask for it in a letter to her brother Richard in 1802. In it she wrote:

"I shall continue to live with my Brother William, but he, having nothing to spare nor being likely to have, at least for many years, I am obliged (I need not say how much he regrets this necessity) to set him aside, and I will consider myself as boarding through my whole life with an indifferent person. Sixty pounds a year is the sum which would entirely gratify all my desires. With sixty pounds a year I should not fear any accidents or changes which might befal me. I cannot look forward to the time when, with my habits of frugality, I could not live comfortably on that sum (Observe I am speaking now, of a provision or settlement for life, and it would be absurd at my age (30 years) to talk of anything else). At present with 60 pounds per ann. I should have something to spare to exercise my better feelings in relieving the necessities of others. I might buy a few books, take a journey now and then — all which things though they do not come under the article of absolute necessaries, you will easily perceive that it is highly desireable that a person of my age and with my education should occasionally have in her power. As to the *mode* of doing this for me, I will say no more than that it seems to be absolutely necessary, to give it any effect, that it should, as much as possible, be independent of accidents of death or any other sort that may befal you or any of my Brothers, its principal object being to make me tranquil in my mind with respect to my future life. Having dealt thus openly with you, my dear Brother, I must add that I should be very loth to be oppressive to you, or any of my Brothers, or to draw upon you for more than you could spare without straightening yourselves — I am sure that John will meet your utmost wishes in the business, and Christopher will do all that he can afford. But when he marries he will be in a different situation from what he is in now, and though he may, and probably will, be as rich, or richer, even as a married man, yet this is uncertain; therefore he may not be able at this present time to make a *permanent* and unconditional engagement. I received 10£ from him the year before last and 20£ last year, and he promised me the same sum annually as long as he should continue a Fellow of Trinity."

Dorothy immersed herself completely in the domestic needs of their life. She papered William's room, hemmed linen by hand, made shifts, shoes and mattresses. Sometimes she ironed the linen all day.

William on the other hand was a keen gardener, attended the well, cut and fetched firewood. Dorothy enjoyed gardening too and together they worked hard to create a pleasant garden from the steep slope which ran straight up from the back door of Dove Cottage. On her walks she often collected ferns and wild plants to plant in the garden. Apart from the ornamental plants, the Wordsworths grew many of the vegetables they needed. Dorothy described her new home and the garden in a letter to Mrs John Marshall, a friend from childhood days, written on September 10th and 12th 1800.

"We have a boat upon the lake and a small orchard and a smaller *garden* which as it is the work of our own hands we regard with pride and partiality. This garden we enclosed from the road and pulled down a fence whch formerly divided it from the orchard. The orchard is very small, but then it is a delightful one from its retirement, and the excessive beauty of the prospect from it. Our cottage is quite large enough for us though very small, and we have made it neat and comfortable within doors and it looks very nice on the outside, for though the roses and honeysuckles which we have planted against it are only of this year's growth yet it is covered all over with green leaves and scarlet flowers for we have trained scarlet beans upon threads which are not only exceedingly beautiful, but very useful, as their produce is immense. The only objection we have to our house is that it is rather too near the road, and from its smallness and the manner in which it is built noises pass from one part of the house to the other, so that if we had any visitors a sick person could not be in quietness. We have made a lodging-room of the parlour below stairs, which has a stone floor therefore we have covered it all over with matting. The bed, though only a camp bed, is large enough for two people to sleep in. We sit in a room above stairs and we have one lodging room with two single beds, a sort of lumber room and a small low unceiled room which I have papered with newspapers and in which we have put a small bed without curtains . . ."

In the orchard there were apple and pear trees. Dorothy "Transplanted raddishes after breakfast" on 16th May 1800,

and "after dinner Aggy weeded onions and carrots." Aggy, the wife of John Fisher, lived nearby.

On 9 June 1800 "W cut down the winter cherry tree. I sowed French Beans and weeded . . . In the evening I stuck peas, watered the garden and planted Brocoli." She also grew kidney beans, spinach, potatoes, turnips and cabbages.

She once wrote that they sometimes found themselves a family of fifteen, and she had to work hard to make their meagre income feed so many. Her brother John, who came to stay with them soon after their arrival, and William caught pike and trout from a boat on the lake to supplement the provisions, and gifts of food from friends sometimes helped.

The Simpsons who lived at High Broadrain on the Keswick road brought them gooseberries, "some large potatoes and plumbs", and pork. Gifts were always reciprocated and Dorothy baked a seed cake for them, took them French Beans and a bag full of peas. Their good friend Mr Griffith sent them a barrel of flour, and Dorothy sent some tea to Mr Cookson of Kendal. From Janet Dockeray she received eggs and milk; gooseberries from Peggy Hodgson; a turkey from Mr Clarkson and nuts from the Baty's. When she cooked a goose for dinner, Dorothy sent some to her poorer neighbour Peggy Ashburner who was ill. In return Peggy sent her "some honey — with a thousand thanks".

In spite of ekeing out the income she was generous to the many travellers and beggars who called at the door.

Apart from sheer economics, their diet was controlled by the seasons to a much greater extent than today. There were no refrigerators or deep freezes in which to preserve food for winter use, and they had to be largely self sufficient. In a remote situation such as Grasmere Dorothy would have to have been adept at baking, pickling, brewing, milking, butter making, candlemaking and a myriad of other household skills lost to many of us today. Goods which could not be bought locally had to be obtained in Kendal, Ambleside or

Windermere. William even had to walk to Ambleside to buy mousetraps. Their coal came by cart from Keswick, and occasionally travellers called selling their wares, "thread, hardware and mustard".

The cool room at Dove Cottage can still be seen today, adjoining the kitchen. It was known as the buttery, and a stream runs beneath the slate flagstones which keeps it cool. There is a slate-topped work table on the right-hand side where hams would have been lain whilst curing, and butter making would have taken place. A cooking range can be seen in the adjoining kitchen, and a pantry.

Dorothy's life was described as one of plain living and high thinking. Her mornings were usually spent baking, but she did have Molly Fisher to help with the housework. To Mrs John Marshall she wrote:

> "Our servant is an old woman 60 years of age whom we took partly out of charity and partly for convenience. She was very ignorant, very foolish and very difficult to teach so that I once almost despaired of her, but the goodness of her dispositions and the great convenience we knew we should find if my perseverance was at last successful induced me to go on. She has now learnt to do everything for us mechanically, except those parts of cooking in which the hands are much employed, for instance she prepares and boils the vegetables and can watch the meat when it is made ready for roasting, looks to the oven etc. My Brother John has been with us 8 months during which time we have had a good deal of company for instance Mary Hutchinson for 5 weeks, Coleridge a month, and Mr and Mrs C and their little boy nearly a month. During all this time we have never hired any helpers either for washing or ironing and she has washed all the linen of all our visitors except the Family of the Coleridges during that month. I help to iron at the great washes about once in 5 weeks, and she washes towels, stockings, waistcoats, petticoats etc. once a week such as do not require much ironing. This she does so quietly in a place apart from the house and we know so little about it as makes it very comfortable. She sleeps at home which is a great convenience in our small house and in winter it is a considerable saving of fire that her home is so near, for after the dishes are washed up, we let the kitchen fire go out and we never light it till it is time to dress the dinner, and she employs herself at home. She is much attached to us and honest and good as ever was a human being."

Molly lived at Sykeside, next to the barn which is now the Wordsworth Museum.

There are many entries in the Journal similar to that of Friday 23rd October 1801, "I baked bread and pies", and although her entries were usually so brief, one is left to wonder what culinary delight she conjured up for William in January 1802 when she wrote, "We had Mr Clarkson's turkey for dinner, the night before we had broiled the gizzard and some mutton and made a nice piece of cookery for Wm's supper . . ."

Cooking methods and equipment in the early part of the nineteenth century were still very basic and certainly not foolproof. There were no temperature controlled ovens and judging whether the oven was hot enough for the dish to be cooked was often done by putting a hand or arm inside, holding it there as long as possible and checking the time it was so held. Perhaps it was the temperature that was wrong on 29th November 1801 when Dorothy "Baked bread, apple pies and giblet pie — a bad giblet pie."

Even the loaves made from the barrel of best American flour sent to them by Mr Griffifth suffered in the baking. According to Molly, the flour required a piping hot oven. The loaves came out burned as black as coal and were not fit to be sent as gifts as William had promised.

The American flour appears to have been a great luxury. Oats and barley rather than wheat had been traditionally grown in the surrounding area, being better suited to the cool wet climate, the short growing season and the poor land. Thus the traditional bread of the Lakeland region was made from oatmeal and was called "haver" bread from the old Norse word "hafrar" meaning oats. It was also called clap bread because the oatmeal and water mixture was clapped or beaten with the hand into a wide thin cake before being cooked on a round iron griddle or "bakstone" over the fire. Wheat flour was more widely available when the Wordsworths lived in Grasmere but flour was often adulterated in the nineteenth century and oatmeal was probably cheaper. Dorothy often ate "hasty pudding" made from oatmeal and boiled salted water, which provided a very cheap meal. Porridge was also part of their staple diet. Once even when travelling they "dined at a publick house on porridge, with a second course of Christmas pies".

Whilst out walking, Dorothy and William often took sandwiches or cold meat with them in their pockets, or when travelling by coach. In 1810 Dorothy described one of her journeys in a letter to William and Sara Hutchinson written from Bury St Edmonds:

"I breakfasted again with the Passengers being determined to take care of myself — we changed coaches at Stamford, and I shared my sandwiches with one of the women and she gave me one of her cakes — so I saved a dinner — and did not drink tea at Huntingdon where the rest had Tea."

She did dine out whilst travelling sometimes however, but she was always mindful of the cost — e.g. at Lincoln, duck and peas, and cream cheese cost two shillings and at Hawes, where she and Mary (William's wife) had tea, William had a partridge and mutton chops and tarts, they were only charged two shillings with a shilling's worth of negus.

On her way home in October 1802 she was "glad to see Stavely it is a place I dearly love to think of — the first mountain village that I came to with Wm when we first began our pilgrimage together. Here we drank a Bason of milk at a publick house . . ."

Breakfast seems to have been a fairly simple meal, for on Sunday morning 14th March 1802 Dorothy noted:

"William had slept badly — he got up at 9 o'clock, but before he rose he had finished the Beggar Boys — and while we were a Breakfast that is (for I had breakfasted) he, with his Basin of Broth before him untouched and a little plate of Bread and butter he wrote the Poem to a Butterfly! He ate not a morsel, nor put on his stockings but sate with his shirt neck unbuttoned, and his waistcoat open while he did it."

Dinner in the middle of the day appears to have been a more substantial meal. Although on 4th March 1802 Dorothy's dinner consisted of two boiled eggs and two apple tarts, they often had some meat such as pork, beefsteak, goose, mutton, turkey or fish with some of their vegetables. During the winter some of their meat may have been dried. Martinmas was the traditional curing period for beef and mutton. This would be dry salt cured, or pickled in brine, and some may have been smoked in the chimney breast. On Sunday mornings it was traditional to boil a cut of meat to be eaten hot for dinner and later cold at subsequent meals. Although fresh meat was by then available all the year round it was probably more expensive than dried meat.

In May 1802 Coleridge came home with them and they had mutton chops and potatoes for supper. Dorothy does not mention any other vegetables and one wonders whether her store of pickled or bottled vegetables had run out. The new season's crops would barely be ready by then. This lack of fresh vegetables, the use of dried meat and an oatmeal diet is believed to have resulted in the frequent internal disorders suffered by many people in the eighteenth and early nineteenth centuries. Perhaps this was a contributory factor to Dorothy's frequent ailments. She often felt sick and unwell and had frequent bowel disorders.

The old herb pudding was the traditional way of providing fresh green foodstuffs in early spring, before the new vegetable crops were ready. It was sometimes known as Easter Ledge pudding and was made with the leaves of Alpine Bistort, groats, young nettles, the leaves of the great bell flower, a few blackcurrant leaves and chives. These would be boiled together in a linen bag and eaten with boiled meat.

In the afternoons they had some tea and with it perhaps some of the cakes Dorothy often baked. In the summer she would take her guests to drink tea in the orchard.

Tea itself was an expensive item. Dorothy ordered some to be sent to her friend Mr Cookson of Kendal from Messrs Twining of London. She ordered 40 pounds of Souchong Tea at seven shillings a pound, Pekoe Tea and one pound of the Best Black tea for a total of £14 12s 6d. There is a delightful reference to the old fashioned way of drinking tea, when William, according to Dorothy, returned home on one occasion in April 1802, "He looked well but was tired and went soon to bed after a dish of Tea."

Tea was not their only drink however — one day she scalded her foot with coffee! After the christening of William's son John they "had a hearty enjoyment of the christening cake, tea and coffee".

Ale was the usual drink in households at that time and the Wordsworths brewed their own. William, however, preferred to drink water. In 1804 Dorothy wrote to Lady Beaumont saying,

> "I wish I could tell you that we had had the pleasure of drinking of the brown Stout. It is not yet tapped, but we are now drinking the last Cask of our own ale. We shall, as you were so good as to direct, put a tea cup full of sweet oil in to the Cask."

Port wine was drunk on Christmas day, and one year they borrowed some bottles for bottling rum. This would have been used to make rum butter, but Mr Simpson once called to drink a glass of rum.

It was a hot day on Tuesday 4th May 1803 when Dorothy and William were out walking. They met Coleridge and rested at a riverside to eat dinner. "I drank a little Brandy and water and was in Heaven," wrote Dorothy. Her euphoria was more likely to have been due to her surroundings and the good company however, rather than the brandy!

Before bedtime, they sometimes had some supper but this seems to have consisted of whatever was left in the larder — broth or bread and butter. On Tuesday night, 11th January 1803, Dorothy had tapioca for her supper, and Mary an egg. William had some cold mutton.

The Journal ends in 1803 but the Wordsworths continued to live at Dove Cottage until 1808 when they moved to Allan Bank. There they kept a cow and two pigs. Dorothy made butter and sold the surplus and the blue milk (the milk from which the cream was taken to make butter). They did not stay long at Allan Bank; the chimneys smoked and keeping the house clean was a constant battle. Although they moved to the Old Vicarage in Grasmere in 1811, this proved to be an unhappy home for them and they moved out of Grasmere in 1813 to Rydal Mount.

There seems little doubt that the Wordsworths were economical due partly to constraints imposed on them by the times in which they lived; their location; initially their finances or perhaps their natural lack of extravagance. Nevertheless, they took full advantage of their own home-grown produce and the local produce. Despite the revolution which the twentieth century has seen in the storage and transportation of food, it is still possible to enjoy the delicious old fashioned types of dishes served in the Wordsworth household and thus have the best of both worlds.

Dorothy's cookery was governed by the seasons and to show her dependence on them, the dishes which she might have cooked, using references from her Grasmere Journals and letters, have been set out according to the appropriate months of the year, starting with May, the month she began her Journal. The recipes have in many cases been based on those contained in nineteenth century cookery books, some even earlier, others are traditional, but nearly all have been modified so that they can be tried at home — with the aid of a temperature controlled oven — a luxury Dorothy could only have dreamed of!

Many of the recipes are quite different from the ones used today, such as the Mountain Mutton and Westmorland Beef. But you too can enjoy a taste of English history by trying the duck with green peas — a combination dating back to the Middle Ages, or by baking one of the very traditional gooseberry puddings.

Nowadays, cooks can buy most of the ingredients needed all the year round in tins or deep frozen. How much better though to use many of them freshly as Dorothy did whenever possible. Fresh young peas or beans just picked that morning, or brown trout, freshly caught in the lake, baked in butter the same day, cannot be bettered. Remember though, the Wordsworths had to pick their peas and catch their fish first! Perhaps you will too!

MAY

·S·BASKERVILLE—MUSCUTT·

"One beautiful view of the Bridge, without St Michael's. Sate down very often, though it was very cold. I resolved to write a journal of the time till W. and J. return."

Batter Pudding

Saturday 29th May 1802
"I made bread and a wee Rhubarb Tart and batter pudding for William."

A batter pudding was either baked in the oven or cooked under the spit in the dripping which fell from the roasting joint, to form Yorkshire pudding.

It is not clear whether William's batter pudding was sweet or savoury. This nineteenth century recipe can be sprinkled with sugar and served with jam sauce or sliced lemons and sugar, or with stewed fruit.

Metric/Imperial	American
900 ml/1½ pints milk	3¾ cups milk
4×15 ml spoons/4 tablespoons plain flour	5 tablespoons all purpose flour
50 g/2 oz butter	½ stick butter
4 eggs	4 eggs
salt	salt
caster sugar	superfine sugar

Mix the flour with a little of the cold milk. Heat the rest of the milk and pour it on the flour, stirring well. Add the butter, eggs and salt. Beat well and put the pudding into a buttered pie dish and bake for 45 minutes at 180°C, 350°F, Gas Mark 4. Turn out and sprinkle with sugar. Serve with jam sauce, lemon juice or stewed fruit.

Rhubarb Tart

Metric/Imperial	American
225 g/8 oz puff pastry	½ lb puff pastry
675 g/1½ lbs rhubarb	1½ lbs rhubarb
100 g/4 oz sugar	½ cup sugar
1×2.5 ml spoon/½ teaspoon powdered cinnamon	½ teaspoon powdered cinnamon

Line a deep pie dish with half the pastry. Wash the rhubarb and wipe dry. If it is old and tough take off the outside skin, otherwise merely cut into smallish pieces and pile into the dish. Sprinkle with sugar and cinnamon and cover with the rest of the pastry. Decorate with the pastry trimmings and cut a slit in the top for the steam to escape. Bake at 220°C, 425°F, Gas Mark 7 for 30 minutes. Sprinkle with a little sugar before serving.

Hasty Pudding

Friday morning 16th May 1800
"After tea went to Ambleside — a pleasant cool but not cold evening. Rydale was very beautiful with spear-shaped streaks of polished steel. No letters! — only one newspaper. I returned by Clappersgate. Grasmere was very solemn in the last glimpse of twilight it calls home the heart to quietness. I had been very melancholy in my walk back. I had many of my saddest thoughts and I could not keep the tears within me. But when I came to Grasmere I felt that it did me good. I finished my letter to M.H.* Ate hasty pudding, and went to bed."
* Mary Hutchinson, later William's wife.

There are numerous recipes for hasty pudding. Sometimes it amounted to no more than a type of porridge made with oatmeal and water.

Oatmeal Hasty Pudding

600 ml/1 pint/2½ cups water
butter
a little salt
oatmeal

Boil the water, add a little salt and a knob of butter. Stir in sufficient to make a thick mixture. Let it boil a few minutes and pour into a serving dish. Dot with pieces of butter, or eat with milk and sugar.

Fine Hasty Pudding

Metric/Imperial	American
600 ml/1 pint milk	2½ cups milk
2 bayleaves	2 bayleaves
4 × 15 ml spoons/4 tablespoons plain flour	5 tablespoons all purpose flour
2 × 15 ml spoons/2 tablespoons sugar	3 tablespoons sugar
25 g/1 oz butter	1 tablespoon butter
salt	salt
1 egg yolk	1 egg yolk

Boil the milk with the bayleaves. Mix the flour, salt and beaten egg yolk until smooth with a little cold milk, and add the hot milk after removing the bayleaves. Let the thickened mixture boil for a few minutes, stirring all the time and pour it into a dish. Dot with pieces of butter.

Bass

Thursday 29th May 1800
"In the morning worked in the garden a little, read King John, Miss Simpson, and Miss Falcon and Mr S came very early. Went to Mr Gell's boat before tea. We fished upon the lake and amongst us caught 13 Bass."

Bass are in fact a sea water fish, but their freshwater cousin the perch are similar in appearance and are prevalent in Grasmere and Rydal. They provide excellent eating, second only to trout, and are usually easy to catch. Their flesh is white, sweet and firm.

Boiled Perch

Remove the guts and the gills, scale and wash well. Lay the fish in slightly salted boiling water and simmer for about 10 minutes or longer if the fish is large. Garnish with parsley and serve with melted butter.

Fried Perch

Clean, skin and fillet the fish. Brush the fillets with beaten egg and cover with breadcrumbs. Fry gently in butter for 5 minutes each side and serve with butter and parsley.

Perch Stewed in Sherry

A few perch depending on size
fish stock
sherry
1 bay leaf
1 clove of garlic
grated nutmeg
small bunch of parsley
2 cloves
salt and pepper
a little flour and butter for thickening
½ teaspoon anchovy sauce

Remove the guts and the gills, scale and wash the fish well. Put them in a pan with enough stock and a glass of sherry to just cover them. Add the bayleaf, garlic, parsley, cloves, salt and simmer for about 10 minutes or until tender depending on the size. When done, take out the fish and strain the liquid. Thicken it with a little flour and butter, pepper, nutmeg and the anchovy sauce, pour over the fish and serve.

JUNE

·S·BASKERVILLE-MUSCUTT·

"We went to R. Newton's for pike floats and went round to Mr Gell's Boat and on to the Lake to fish. We caught nothing — it was extremely cold. The Reeds and Bulrushes or Bullpipes of a tender soft green . . ."

Boiled Pike

Thursday 14th June 1800
"William and I went upon the water to set pike floats. John fished under Loughrigg. We returned to dinner, 2 pikes boiled and roasted."

1 pike about 3 kg/7 lbs in weight
salt
a little vinegar
1 onion sliced
1 blade of mace
6 black peppercorns
1 bayleaf
parsley and lemon thyme

Pour boiling water over the fish until the scales go dull. Put the fish in cold water and scrape off the scales with the back of a knife. Gut and clean the fish and put it in a fish kettle with the other ingredients. If a round pan is used, secure the tail of the fish with a skewer in the mouth in the traditional manner. Add just enough water to cover, and bring to the boil. Simmer gently for 6–8 minutes per pound (½ kg) according to the thickness of the fish. Serve with plain melted butter or Dutch Sauce.

Dutch Sauce

Metric/Imperial	American
1×2.5 ml spoon/½ teaspoon plain flour	½ teaspoon all purpose flour
50 g/2 oz butter	½ stick butter
4×15 ml spoons/tablespoons tarragon vinegar	5 tablespoons tarragon vinegar
2 egg yolks	2 egg yolks
juice of half a lemon	juice of half a lemon
salt to taste	salt to taste

Heat, but do not boil, all the ingredients except the lemon juice in a pan stirring all the time until it thickens. If it curdles, strain it through muslin. Add the lemon juice and serve.

Baked Gooseberry Pudding

Saturday 7th June 1800
"A very warm cloudy morning, threatening to rain. I walked up to Mr Simpson's to gather gooseberries — it was a very fine afternoon. Little Tommy came down with me, ate gooseberry pudding and drank tea with me."

Metric/Imperial	American
600 ml/1 pint cooked pulped gooseberries	2½ cups cooked pulped gooseberries
225 g/8 oz puff pastry	½ lb puff pastry
3 eggs	3 eggs
40 g/1½ oz butter	2 tablespoons butter
100 g/4 oz breadcrumbs	2 cups breadcrumbs
sugar to taste	sugar to taste

Beat the eggs well and add to the gooseberry pulp together with the butter, breadcrumbs and sugar to taste. Beat the mixture well. Line a pie or flan dish with the puff pastry and put in the mixture. Bake for about 40 minutes at 200°C, 400°F, Gas Mark 6. Dredge with caster sugar (superfine sugar) and serve. Serves 4 or 5.

French Beans or Young Runner Beans

Dorothy trained scarlet beans around the cottage at Town End as much for their pretty flowers and leaves as the beans.

Metric/Imperial	American
1 kg/2 lbs french beans	2 lbs french beans
150 ml/¼ pint white or brown stock	⅔ cup white or brown stock
25 g/1 oz butter	1 tablespoon butter
25 g/1 oz plain flour	¼ cup all purpose flour
2×15 ml spoons/2 tablespoons double cream	3 tablespoons heavy cream
salt and pepper	salt and pepper
a little grated nutmeg	a little grated nutmeg

Remove the strings and the stalks from the beans and cut them diagonally into four. Put them into the boiling stock and cook for 5 to ten minutes until tender. Melt the butter in another pan and add the flour to make a roux. Gradually add the stock from the beans and stir to make a smooth sauce. Add the drained beans and stir in the cream. Add the nutmeg, salt and pepper and serve.

Summer Fruit and Salads

Tuesday 15th June 1802
*"A sweet grey mild morning. The birds sing soft and low . . .
After William rose we went and sate in the orchard till dinner
time. We walked a long time in the Evening upon our favourite
path . . . Came in. There was a Basket of Lettuces, . . ."*

*With the fresh lettuce for dinner, they may have had some of
the "Raddishes" which Dorothy had transplanted in May, and
some hard boiled eggs or cold meat, perhaps with some
mustard bought from a traveller.*

*On Sunday morning 26th July 1800 she rows down to
Loughrigg Fell, visited the white foxglove, gathered wild
strawberries, and walked up to view Rydale. It seems doubtful
whether the strawberries ever reached the dinner table, but
with raspberries, rhubarb, "very fine gooseberries", and black
cherries there were plenty of fresh fruits and vegetables to
choose from in the summer months.*

Lemon-thyme Vinegar

Tuesday 24th June 1800
*"W. and I drank tea at Mr Simpson's. Brought down Lemon-
Thyme, greens, etc. . ."*

Lemon-thyme
white vinegar

Bruise the leaves of the lemon-thyme with a rolling pin and half
fill jars with them. Fill with cold vinegar and store for 6 weeks,
shaking the bottles daily if possible. Strain the vinegar through
fine muslin until clear and rebottle.
    This can be used in salad dressings.

*Dorothy grew lemon-thyme in the garden for on Wednesday
4th June she wrote, "I walked to the lake-side in the morning,
took up plants and sate upon a stone reading Ballads. In the
Evening I was watering plants when Mr and Miss Simpson
called. I accompanied them home, and we went to the
waterfall at the head of the valley. It was very interesting in the
Twilight. I brought home lemon thyme and several other
plants, and planted them by moonlight."*

JULY

·S·BASKERVILLE-MUSCUTT·

"The Evening excessively beautiful — a rich reflection of the moon, the moonlight clouds and the hills, and from the Rays gap a huge rainbow pillar."

Cumberland Currant Cake

Metric/Imperial	American
225 g/8 oz plain flour	2 cups all purpose flour
pinch of salt	pinch of salt
100 g/4 oz butter	1 stick butter
30 ml/2 tablespoons cold water	3 tablespoons cold water
25 g/1 oz sugar	2 tablespoons sugar
*	*
225 g/8 oz currants	1½ cups currants
100 g/4 oz sugar	½ cup sugar
3×15 ml spoons/3 table- spoons rum	4 tablespoons rum

Warm the rum and pour over the currants to make them swell. To make the pastry, mix the flour and salt in a basin and rub in the butter until it looks like breadcrumbs. Add the water and with a knife, stir the mixture until it forms a stiff paste. Turn out onto a floured board and divide into two equal pieces. Roll out both portions to fit a shallow tin e.g. a swiss roll tin. Place half the pastry in the tin. Drain the currants well and spread over the pastry evenly. Sprinkle with the sugar and the rum. Cover the currants with the pastry and seal the edges. Brush the surface with milk and bake at 220°C, 425°F, Gas Mark 7 for about 30 minutes or until golden brown. Allow to cool and cut into squares. Dredge with caster sugar (superfine sugar).

Mushroom Ketchup

The recipe given for Beefsteaks by Mrs Beeton in 1861 suggested that they be served on a very hot dish into which she had put a tablespoon of mushroom ketchup.

According to an old cookery book, this sauce is of Japanese origin. Its name according to English spelling, ketchup or catsup, is derived from the Japanese "kitjap".

3 kg/7 lbs mushrooms
225 g/½ lb salt

For every 600 ml/pint/2½ cups of juice:
6 cloves
25 g/1 oz/¼ cup salt
1×2.5 ml spoon/½ teaspoon of peppercorns
1×2.5 ml spoon/½ teaspoon ground ginger

Put the roughly chopped and cleaned mushrooms into a large bowl in layers, sprinkling salt between each layer. Let it stand for two or three days. Press the juice from the mushrooms and strain it into a pan. For every pint (or equivalent) measure of juice add the cloves, salt, peppercorns and ginger as appropriate. Bring the mixture to the boil and let it simmer for about half an hour. Strain through a fine sieve, and when cold, bottle it.

Veal Pie

Saturday July 3rd 1802
"I breakfasted in bed, being not very well. Aggy Ashburner helped Molly with the Linen. I made veal and gooseberry pies. It was very cold. Thomas Ashburner went for coals for us. There was snow upon the mountain tops."

Metric/Imperial	American
1 kg/2 lbs veal	2 lbs veal
100 g/4 oz chopped ham or bacon	¼ lb chopped ham or bacon
pepper and salt	pepper and salt
1 × 15 ml spoon/1 tablespoon mixed savoury herbs	1 tablespoon mixed savoury herbs
a little powdered mace	a little powdered mace
a little gravy	a little gravy
yolks of two hard boiled eggs	yolks of two hard boiled eggs
grated peel of 1 lemon	grated peel of 1 lemon

for the pastry:	
225 g/8 oz plain flour	2 cups all purpose flour
pinch of salt	pinch of salt
100 g/4 oz butter	1 stick butter
cold water a little beaten egg to mix	cold water a little beaten egg to mix

Make the pastry by rubbing the fat into the flour and salt until the mixture resembles breadcrumbs. Add a little water and with a knife, stir until it forms a stiff paste. Roll out and line a pie dish with two thirds of the pastry.

Chop up the veal and season it with salt, pepper and mace. Add the chopped ham or bacon, chopped egg yolks, lemon peel and herbs and mix well. Put into the pie dish with just a little water or stock to moisten it. Place a pie funnel in the middle and cover the pie with a pastry lid. Decorate it with pastry leaves and brush with beaten egg. Bake for about 1½ hours at 200°C, 400°F, Gas Mark 6, covering with foil if it begins to brown too much. Add the heated gravy through the pie funnel after baking.

Stewed Duck with Green Peas

On Tuesday 26th July 1802 Dorothy was at Hull in Yorkshire. "Market day. Streets dirty, very rainy, did not leave Hull till 4 o'clock, and left Barton at about 6 — rained all the way almost. A beautiful village at the foot of a hill with trees — a gentleman's house converted into a Lady's Boarding school. We had a woman in bad health in the coach, and took in a Lady and her Daughter — supped at Lincoln. Duck and peas, and cream cheese — paid 2/-."

It was traditional to serve duck with green peas, and this recipe uses cold roast duck.

The remains of cold roast duck
50 g/2 oz/½ stick butter
3 or 4 slices of lean ham or bacon
1×15 ml spoon/1 tablespoon flour
1.2 litres/2 pints/5 cups thin gravy
small bunch of spring onions
sprigs of parsley
3 cloves
225 g/½ lb young green peas
cayenne pepper and salt to taste
1×5 ml spoon/1 teaspoon caster sugar (superfine)

Sauté the chunks of duck meat in melted butter together with the chopped ham or bacon. Sprinkle with the flour and stir it in well before adding the gravy. Add the chopped onions, cloves, chopped parsley and simmer gently for 15 minutes. Add the green peas and stew gently for about half an hour. Season with cayenne, salt and sugar.

AUGUST

·S·BASKERVILLE-MUSCUTT·

"We then went to peep into Langdale. The Pikes were very grand. We walked back to the view of Rydale, which was now a dark mirror."

Gooseberry Pie

On Thursday morning 7th August 1800 Dorothy "Packed up the mattrass, and sent to Keswick. Boiled gooseberries — N.B. 2 lbs of sugar in the first panfull, 3 quarts all good measure — 3 lbs in the 2nd 4 quarts — 2½ lbs in the 3rd. A very fine day. William composing in the wood in the morning. In the evening we walked to Mary Point. A very fine sunset."

This reference to preserving gooseberries is the nearest thing Dorothy gives to a recipe in her journal! Whilst she would have used preserved gooseberries in the winter for her pies, she also made fresh gooseberry pies on Saturday July 3rd 1802.

Metric/Imperial	American
225 g/8 oz plain flour	2 cups all purpose flour
pinch of salt	pinch of salt
100 g/4 oz butter	1 stick butter
25 g/1 oz sugar	2 tablespoons sugar
cold water to mix	cold water to mix
675 g/1½ lbs gooseberries	1½ lbs gooseberries
100 g/4 oz sugar if raw fruit used	½ cup sugar if raw fruit used

With a pair of scissors, top and tail the gooseberries, mix them with the 4 oz sugar and put them into a 1 litre/2 pint buttered pie dish, piling the fruit high in the middle, or use a pie funnel. Make the pastry using 1 oz of sugar, and line the edge of the dish with a strip of pastry. Put on the pastry cover, trim off the excess and decorate the edges of the pie. Put two slits in the centre of the pie if no pie funnel is used, to allow the steam to escape. Brush the pie top with some cold milk and sprinkle with sugar. Bake at 200°C, 400°F, Gas Mark 6 for 30-40 minutes.

Baked Stuffed Pike

Sunday Morning 3rd August 1800
"I made pies and stuffed the pike — baked a loaf."

Metric/Imperial	American
1 or 2 pike	1 or 2 pike
1 egg	1 egg
breadcrumbs	breadcrumbs
100 g/4oz butter	1 stick butter

For the Forcemeat:	For the Forcemeat:
25 g/1 oz butter	1 tablespoon butter
25 g/1 oz shredded suet	3 tablespoons shredded suet
1 teaspoon minced savoury herbs including parsley	1 teaspoon minced savoury herbs including parsley
25 g/1 oz bacon fat	1 tablespoon bacon fat
a little finely sliced onion	a little finely sliced onion
salt, nutmeg and cayenne	salt, nutmeg and cayenne
100 g/4 oz breadcrumbs	2 cups breadcrumbs
1 egg well beaten	1 egg well beaten

Scale the fish, take out the guts and gills, wash and wipe it thoroughly dry. To make the forcemeat, mix all the ingredients together well, binding it together with the beaten egg. Stuff the pike with the forcemeat and sew it up. Brush it over with egg, sprinkle with breadcrumbs and baste with butter before putting it in a hot oven — 200°C, 400°F, Gas Mark 6 for 35 minutes or more depending on the size of the fish. If the fish begins to colour too much, cover it with foil. Test with a skewer. The flesh should move easily from the backbone.

Green Peas with Cream

On Sunday Morning 3rd August 1800
"I made pies and stuffed the pike — baked a loaf. Headache after dinner — I lay down . . . Peas for dinner."

The peas were obviously fresh from the garden for the next day she also *"pulled a large basket of peas"*. Peas should be picked and shelled just before they are to be eaten to be enjoyed at their best.

Put the shelled peas into fast boiling slightly salted water to which just a little sugar has been added. A sprig of mint can also be added. Boil for 10-15 minutes until tender. Drain and serve with a knob of butter.

Hannah Glasse's eighteenth century recipe for green peas with cream needs no modification:

"Take a quart[1] of fine green peas, put them in a stewpan with a piece of butter as big as an egg, rolled in a little flour, season them with salt and nutmeg, a bit of sugar as big as a nutmeg, a little bundle of sweet herbs[2], some parsley chopped fine, a quarter of a pint[3] of boiling water. Cover them close, and let them stew very softly half an hour, then pour on a quarter of a pint of good cream[4]. Give it one boil and serve it up for a side plate."

1   about 650 g/1½ lbs
2   e.g mint, sage, marjoram as available
3   150 ml/⅔ cup
4   double or heavy cream

Pan Roasted New Potatoes

Friday May 14th 1802
"A very cold morning — hail and snow showers all day . . . After tea I walked to Rydale for Letters . . . I walked as fast as I could back again with my letter from S.H. which I skimmed over at Tommy Fleming's. Met Wm at the top of White Moss. We walked a little beyond Olliffs.* Near 10 when we came in. Wm and Molly had dug the ground and planted potatoes in my absence . . ."
* The Olliffs lived at The Hollins on the road to Keswick.

This recipe needs young, round, even sized potatoes which would be ready by August.

Wash 450 g/1 lb of potatoes and put them in a thick bottomed pan with 50 g/2 oz/½ stick of butter, salt to taste, and cover tightly. Place the pan over a low heat and shake occasionally, but do not remove the cover. After ¾ hour, the potatoes will have a brown crust but inside they will be white and tender.

Salted Beans

Saturday 22nd August 1800
"A very fine morning. Wm was composing all the morning. I shelled peas, gathered beans, and worked in the garden till ½ past 12 then walked with William in the wood."

To preserve the beans for use in the winter Dorothy would have picked them when they were young and tender. For 3 lbs/ 1½ kg of beans she would have needed 1 lb/½ kg of kitchen salt (not the free flowing table salt).

Wash, dry and de-string the beans. Slice runner beans, but leave french beans whole. Place a layer of salt in a glass jar and then a layer of beans. Continue to fill the jar with alternate layers. Press the beans down well and finish with salt. Cover and leave for a few days. As the beans shrink, top up the jar with more beans and salt. Leave the brine which forms in the jar as this acts as a preservative. Seal the jar. Do not economise on the salt otherwise the beans may deteriorate.

When ready to use the beans, wash them well in several changes of water. Soak them for 2 hours in warm water. Cook them in boiling water until tender. Drain and serve as usual with a knob of butter or add a sprinkling of grated nutmeg.

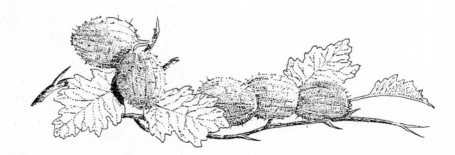

SEPTEMBER

"*After dinner Coleridge discovered a rock seat in the orchard . . .*"

·S·BASKERVILLE·MUSCUTT·

Mountain Mutton and Westmorland Beef

18th September 1818 — Dorothy wrote to Mrs Thomas Clarkson:
"I found all at dinner except Mr W.* and his two youngest sons who were not come. Mrs W. looked very interesting, for she was full of delight and talked as fast as any of the young ones — but I must say that she has never since appeared to me to such advantage. Yet I like her very well — admire her goodness and patience and meekness — but that slowness and whininess of manner — tending to selfrighteousness, I do not like. Not a particle of this was visible that first day when they were all rejoicing over their dinner of Mountain Mutton and Westmorland Beef — and each telling, — and all at once — his or her separate feelings."
* William Wilberforce, M.P.

Mutton and beef were cooked and eaten together in the eighteenth century and make an unusual dish for a large dinner party. As the Wordsworths often had a large number to feed this would have been ideal.

1½ kg/4 lbs of mutton or lamb
1 kg/2 lbs piece of rump of beef prepared for roasting
2 bouquet garnis
parsley
a little seasoned flour
a large onion stuck with some cloves
2 blades mace
some whole peppercorns
100 g/4 oz/1 stick butter

For the sauce:
4 lambs kidneys
350 g/¾ lb small mushrooms
a glass of red wine
100 g/4 oz/1 cup plain flour (all purpose)
stock from the meat pan
salt and pepper
lemon juice
lemon slices
parsley

Prepare both joints as for roasting, trimming off any surplus fat. Roll each joint in the seasoned flour and brown each one in a little butter in a frying pan. Place both joints side by side in a large cooking vessel on top of the cooker with the onion, bouquet garnis, peppercorns, mace and a little salt. Add enough water to cover both joints and bring slowly to the boil. Reduce the heat and simmer for two hours with the lid on.

Shortly before the meats have finished cooking the sauce can be made. The kidneys should be skinned, halved and fried in butter in a large deep pan. Lift them out and saute the mushrooms, adding a little more butter if necessary. Put the kidneys back into the pan with the mushrooms and the red wine. Add about 450 ml/1 pint/2½ cups of stock from the meat pan and simmer for a few minutes until the kidneys are cooked. Drain the kidneys and mushrooms, returning the liquid to the pan. Mix the flour with a little cold water and gradually add about a pint/450 ml/2½ cups of stock from the meat pan, stirring briskly to ensure a smooth consistency. Add to the kidney and mushroom liquid and cook until a thick gravy consistency is achieved. Season to taste, adding a little lemon juice if wished. Add the mushrooms and kidneys and warm them through.

Drain the joints of meat and carve the beef. Arrange the

slices round the edge of a large deep serving dish, setting the lamb joint whole, in the middle. Pour the gravy over the beef and garnish with plenty of parsley and a few lemon slices.

Serves at least 8.

Mutton Chops

Monday Morning 1st September 1800
"I broiled Coleridge a mutton chop which he ate in bed."

With so many sheep in the lakeland area, mutton chops were a frequently eaten dish. This old recipe uses mint and parsley — herbs which the Wordsworths were likely to have grown in their garden.

4 mutton or lamb chops
salt and pepper
50 g/2 oz/½ stick butter
2 tablespoons fresh chopped mint *
2 tablespoons fresh chopped parsley *
plenty of hot mashed potatoes
* use less if using dried herbs

Mix the chopped herbs and butter together well. Cut a large slit in the lean part of each chop and stuff the butter mixture into it. Grill the chops for 7 or 8 minutes each side. Have ready a large quantity of hot well mashed potatoes and pile these into the centre of a serving dish to form a steep mound. When the chops are ready, place these in a circle, arranged vertically, round the potato, thick end downwards. Sprinkle with chopped parsley and serve hot.

Dumplings

On September 9th 1800 Dorothy's brothers accompanied John Marshall "round the two lakes, Rydale and Grasmere, by which means he saw them in many new points of view and in much greater beauty than he had seen them before. I was left at home to make pies and dumplings, and was to follow them when I had finished my business, but as they could not tell me exactly which way they should go I sought them in vain, and after we had all walked far enough to get very good appetites we met together at two o'clock at our own house to dinner."

Perhaps she was boiling a piece of beef for them with dumplings followed by apple pie. Hardly anyone can resist dumplings and they would have been ideal for those hearty appetites.

Metric/Imperial	American
225 g/8 oz self raising flour	2 cups self-rising flour
100 g/4 oz shredded suet	½ cup shredded suet
a pinch of salt	a pinch of salt
125 ml/¼ pint milk and water	⅔ cup milk and water

Mix the flour, salt and suet in a bowl and stir in the liquid gradually, to make a pliable dough. It should not be too wet. Turn the dough out on to a floured board and knead lightly. Allow to rest for a few minutes. Roll into small balls about 2.5 cm/1 inch thick. Drop these into the simmering stock 20 minutes before the meat should be ready, or they can be added to a stew 20 minutes before it has finished cooking. Lift out of the stockpan very carefully as they are fragile. Arrange round the edges of the boiled beef and sprinkle with parsley.

Roast Venison

One September Saturday in 1819, two Mr Jacksons and Mr Gee dined with the Wordsworths upon venison and partridges from Lowther.

Venison should be hung in a cool place for about two weeks, and then wiped over with a damp cloth. If the meat is from an older animal it will benefit from a marinade for a couple of days. Younger animals can be cooked without.

1 shoulder, haunch or saddle of venison about 2.3 kg/5 lbs
olive oil
a little flour

For the marinade:
750 ml/1½ pints/3¾ cups red wine
250 ml/½ pint/1¼ cups cooking oil
a clove of garlic, crushed
1 sliced onion
1 bouquet garni
a few whole black peppercorns
olive oil

To make the marinade, mix all the ingredients together except the olive oil and pour over the meat into a deep dish. Leave in a cool place for about two days, turning the joint frequently. Afterwards, lift out the meat and pat it dry before rubbing all over with the olive oil. Wrap it in foil and roast in a preheated oven at 190°C, 375°F, Gas Mark 5 for 35 minutes per pound/½ kg. Remove the joint from the foil and make the gravy from the juices and the original marinade, thickening it with a little flour. Check the seasonings and simmer for a few minutes. Serve with redcurrant jelly. Serves about 10 people.

Creamed Spinach

The spinach which Dorothy sowed on 13th June 1800 would have been ready for picking by September.

1 kg/2 lb fresh spinach
a large knob of butter
salt and pepper
a pinch of grated nutmeg
150 ml/¼ pint/⅔ cup single (light) cream
croutons of fried bread

Remove the stalks and any damaged leaves, and wash thoroughly to remove any dirt. Place in a large pan without any extra water and cook slowly until the spinach has reduced in volume and made it own juice. Add salt and pepper and continue cooking slowly for another 5 minutes. Drain thoroughly, removing as much liquid as possible and chop. Melt the butter in a saucepan, add the chopped spinach and nutmeg, and cook until heated through. Add the cream and stir well. Serve with croutons of fried bread.

OCTOBER

"S·BASKERVILLE-MUSCUTT"

"After dinner we walked round Rydale Lake, rich, calm, streaked, very beautiful."

Roast Partridge

In October 1802 Dorothy, William and Mary Hutchinson were travelling in Yorkshire. *"At our return to the Inn we found new horses and a new Driver, and we went on nicely to Hawes where we arrived before it was quite dark. Mary and I got tea, and William had a partridge and mutton chops for his supper. Mary sate down with him. We had also a shilling's worth of negus and Mary made me some Broth for all which supper we were only charged 2/-."*

One nineteenth century recipe suggests broiled partridge is suitable for a luncheon, breakfast or supper dish — as William discovered. One should "Broil them over a very clear fire and dish them on a hot dish; rub a small piece of butter over each half and send them to the table with brown gravy or mushroom sauce."
  Partridges should be hung for a few days before being plucked, drawn and trussed. Young birds are best for roasting.

4 young birds (1 per person)
butter
4 slices of salt pork or streaky bacon
salt
4 slices of toast
1 lemon
watercress

Place a knob of butter and a sprinkling of salt inside each cleaned bird. Place the strips of bacon or pork over the breasts. Put each bird on top of a piece of toast in a roasting tin and cook at 220°C, 425°F, Gas Mark 7 for 20 minutes, basting frequently. Remove the bacon or pork for the last few minutes and sprinkle the breasts with flour. Cook until brown. Serve each bird whole (if not too big) on its piece of toast garnished with lemon wedges, watercress and gravy.

Negus

There are various recipes for negus; here is just one.

Extract the juice of one lemon and cut two others into thin slices. Take four glasses of melted calves-foot jelly, sweetened and spiced (with nutmeg) to taste. Pour 1 litre/2 pints/5 cups of boiling water on to these ingredients in a deep jug, cover and stand for 20 minutes. Add one bottleful of white wine.

Elderberry Cake

Saturday 16th October 1802 — "Mary and I had a pleasant walk, the day was very bright, the people busy getting in their corn — reached home about 5 o'clock. I was not quite well but better after tea. We made cakes, etc."

Dorothy does not specify what kinds of cakes she baked. Perhaps one was this elderberry cake.

Metric/Imperial	American
225 g/8 oz ripe elderberries*	½ lb ripe elderberries*
75 g/3 oz sugar	⅓ cup sugar
For the pastry:	For the pastry:
200 g/8 oz plain flour	2 cups all purpose flour
100 g/4 oz butter	1 stick butter
pinch of salt	pinch of salt
30 ml/2 tablespoons cold water	3 tablespoons cold water
25 g/1 oz sugar	3 tablespoons sugar
For the icing:	For the icing:
100 g/4 oz sieved icing sugar	½ cup confectioners sugar
1 x 15 ml spoon/1 tablespoon warm water	2 tablespoons warm water

Wash the elderberries, remove any stalks, allow to dry and toss in sugar. Make the pastry by mixing the flour and salt together, then rub in the fat until the mixture looks like breadcrumbs. Add the sugar and then the cold water. With a knife, stir the mixture until it forms a stiff paste. Pull together and form into a ball. Divide into two equal parts. Roll out one half on a floured board, and use to line a pie plate or shallow tin. Cover it with elderberries and sprinkle sugar over. Wet the edges with water. Roll out the other half of the pastry and cover the elderberries with it. Seal the edges. Bake at 220°C, 425°F, Gas Mark 7 for about 30 minutes.

When cool, dust with a thick layer of icing sugar or cover with thin sugar icing. To make this, put the icing sugar and warm water in a bowl and stir until smooth. Pour over the cake and leave it to set.

*Elderberries are ripe when the tassels hang downwards.

Giblet Pie

Tuesday 29th October 1800
"A very rainy night. I was baking bread in the morning and made a giblet pie."

1 set of duck or goose giblets
450 g/1 lb rumpsteak
1 onion
plenty of freshly ground black pepper
a bunch of savoury herbs
pastry
600 ml/1 pint/2½ cups water.

Clean and put the giblets in a pan with the onion, pepper and herbs. Add the water and simmer gently for ½ hour. Drain the giblets etc. but retain the liquid. Let them cool and cut them into pieces. Line the bottom of a pie dish with a few pieces of rumpsteak, add a layer of giblets/onion and more steak on top. Season with salt and pepper and pour on the strained gravy in which the giblets were stewed. Cover with pastry and bake for just over 1½ hours in a preheated oven at 220°C, 425°F, Gas Mark 7. Cover the pastry with foil to prevent it browning too much.

Pickled Plums

Wednesday Morning 22nd October 1800
"In the evening Stoddart* came in when we were at tea, and after tea Mr and Miss Simpson with large potatoes and plumbs . . ."

* Sir John Stoddart

Metric/Imperial	American
1½ kg/3 lbs plums	3 lbs plums
900 g/2 lbs demerara sugar	2 lbs demerara sugar
750 ml/1¼ pints vinegar	3¼ cups vinegar
one clove per plum	one clove per plum
5 cm/2 inches cinnamon stick	2 inches cinnamon stick

Heat the vinegar with the cinnamon stick gently in a large pan and add the sugar, stirring until dissolved. Turn off the heat. Remove any plum stems, wash and dry the plums and press a clove into the end of each. Add the plums to the vinegar mixture and bring to the boil slowly. Lower the heat and simmer very gently until tender. Stir as little as possible so as not to break the skins. Allow to cool in the liquid and lift out. Boil the liquid for about 10 minutes to reduce and allow to cool. Put the plums and liquid in sterilised jars and cover. Leave for about three months to mature before using with cold ham or beef.

Sloe and Apple Jelly

Sloes grow well in the Lake District and on Thursday 6th May 1802, Dorothy remarked on the Sloe-thorns in the hedges. The fruits are ready in October and are bitter, but they make a tangy jelly. They need to be combined with apples to give a good set.

450 g/1 lb sloes
450 g/1 lb apples
450 g/1 lb/2 cups of sugar for each 600 ml/1 pint/2½ cups juice

Wash the sloes and apples. Prick the sloes, and cut the apples into rough chunks without peeling or coring. Put both fruits into one pan and add just enough water to cover. Gradually bring to the boil and simmer until pulped. Put the mixture in a jelly bag and leave to drip overnight. Measure the juice back into a pan and add 450 g/1 lb/2 cups sugar for every pint or equivalent measure of juice. Simmer until the sugar dissolves, then boil rapidly for 10 minutes or longer until a set is obtained. Pour into small warmed and sterilised jars and cover at once.

NOVEMBER

·S·BASKERVILLE-MUSCUTT·

"Wm and Mary walked to Rydale . . . The Lakes beautiful. The Church an image of peace."

Roast Goose

Thursday 12th November 1801
"A beautiful still sunshiny morning. We rose very late. I put the rag Boxes into order. We walked out while the Goose was roasting."

1 goose (allow 350 g /¾ lb per person when buying)

For the stuffing:
4 large onions
2 x 5 ml spoons/2 teaspoons crushed sage
100 g/4 oz/2 cups breadcrumbs
45 g/1½ oz/2 tablespoons butter
seasoned flour i.e. flour, salt and pepper mixed
1 beaten egg

To make the stuffing, peel and slice the onions, and put them into boiling water. Simmer for 10 minutes, strain and chop them. Add the sage, breadcrumbs and egg and mix well. Use to stuff the goose from the neck end. Truss the bird and put on a grid in a roasting tin. Rub lightly with seasoned flour and cover with foil. Roast for 25 minutes per 450 g/pound at 180°C, 350°F, Gas Mark 4. During the last half hour remove the foil to allow the bird to brown.

To make the gravy, simmer the giblets in water for about an hour, allow to cool and remove the excess fat. Pour off the fat from the roasting pan juices and use the stock to make the gravy, thickening if necessary. Serve with gooseberry sauce.

Gooseberry Sauce

Metric/Imperial	American
200 g/8 oz gooseberries	½ lb gooseberries
150 ml/¼ pint water	⅔ cup water
50 g/2 oz sugar	⅓ cup sugar
25 g/1 oz butter	1 tablespoon butter

With a pair of scissors, top and tail the gooseberries, wash them and put into a pan with the water. Cover and simmer until the fruit is soft and pulped. Add the sugar and then sieve the mixture. Return to the pan with the butter and reheat gently.

Turnips with Parsley Sauce

Turnips store well during the winter and those which Molly weeded on Monday May 19th 1800 would probably have been kept to supplement the winter diet when most fresh vegetables were unobtainable.

Metric/Imperial	American
675 g/1 ½ lbs small turnips	1 ½ lbs small turnips
50 g/2 oz butter	½ stick butter
300 ml/½ pint weak stock	1 ¼ cups weak stock
pepper and salt	pepper and salt
chopped parsley	chopped parsley
1 x 15 ml spoon/1 tablespoon flour	1 tablespoon all purpose flour

Melt half the butter in a pan and add the peeled and diced turnips. Season with salt and pepper. Toss them for a few minutes then add the stock and simmer until tender. In another pan, melt the rest of the butter and add the flour. Gradually blend in the stock from the turnip pan. Add the turnips and chopped parsley and simmer for a few minutes until the sauce is cooked. Serve with boiled mutton.

Apple Pie

Wednesday 25th November 1801
"It rained a little and rained afterwards all the afternoon. I baked pies and bread, and wrote to Sara Hutchinson and Coleridge."

On the following day "Mr. Olliff called before Wm was up to say that they would drink tea with us this afternoon. We walked into Easedale to gather mosses and to fetch cream. I went for the cream and they sate under a wall. It was piercing cold and a hail storm came on in the afternoon. The Ollifs arrived at 5 o'clock."

Perhaps they had the cream with apple pie.

Metric/Imperial	American
450 g/1 lb shortcrust pastry	1 lb pie dough
¾ kg/1 ½ lb cooking apples	1 ½ lbs tart apples
75 g/3 oz sugar	⅓ cup sugar
(or use honey to sweeten)	(or use honey to sweeten)
1 x 5 ml spoon/1 teaspoon grated lemon rind	1 teaspoon grated lemon rind
caster sugar	superfine sugar

Peel, core and slice the apples and simmer with just a little water in a pan until soft. Add the lemon rind and sweeten to taste. Allow to cool. The mixture should not be too wet. Prepare the pastry and divide into two. Roll out half to fit an ovenproof pie plate and spoon the cooled apple apple evenly over the pastry. Moisten the edges of the pastry with a little cold water and cover with the pastry lid. Trim the edges and decorate the top with pastry trimmings. Put a slit in the centre to allow the steam to escape. Brush with beaten egg or milk and cook in a preheated oven at 200°C, 400°F, Gas Mark 6 for about 30 minutes until golden brown. Dust with caster sugar (superfine sugar) before serving.

Parkins

Thursday 6th November 1800
"A very rainy morning and night. I was baking bread dinner and parkins".

Parkins were traditionally eaten in Yorkshire in November, and as Dorothy spent much of her youth in Halifax she probably learned how to make them whilst there.

Metric/Imperial	American
150 g/6 oz plain flour	1½ cups all purpose flour
75 g/3 oz brown sugar	⅓ cup moist sugar
50 g/2 oz medium oatmeal	½ cup medium oatmeal
75 g/3 oz butter	¾ stick butter
100 g/4 oz golden syrup	¼ lb light corn syrup
1 egg	1 egg
1 x 5 ml spoon/1 teaspoon ground ginger	1 teaspoon powdered ginger
1½ x 5 ml spoons/1½ teaspoons bicarbonate of soda	1½ teaspoons baking soda
milk	milk
a large pinch of powdered cinnamon	a large pinch of powdered cinnamon

Sift the flour, ginger, cinnamon, bicarbonate of soda (baking soda) together in a bowl and add the oatmeal. Melt the sugar, margarine and syrup slowly in a pan and when well mixed, pour over the dry ingredients. Add the beaten egg and mix well using a little milk to form a fairly soft runny mixture. Pour into a square or oblong cake tin lined with greaseproof paper which has been greased and bake at 160°C, 325°F, Gas Mark 3 for 1 hour. Cool on a wire rack and when quite cold, usually the following day, cut into squares.

Roasted Onions

The onions which Aggy Fisher weeded on Friday 16th May 1800 for Dorothy would have been stored for use in the winter.

Nowadays people peel and parboil onions before roasting them, but they can be delicious cooked with their skins on. This improves their flavour and the skins go crispy.

Wash and dry one unskinned onion per person and place in an ovenproof dish. Pour over 3 or 4 tablespoons of melted lard or dripping and ensure they are well coated. Roast at 190°C, 375°F, Gas Mark 5 for about 45 minutes or until tender. Season with salt and pepper.

DECEMBER

·S·BASKERVILLE-MUSCUTT·

"Supped upon a hare."

Roasted Apples

Monday 28th December 1801
"William, Mary and I set off on foot to Keswick. We carried some cold mutton in our pockets, and dined at John Stanley's* where they were making Christmas pies . . . There we roasted apples in the oven."

* Landlord of the King's Head at Thirlspot on the road to Keswick.

Instead of plain baking, try baking apples with rum butter. Wash and core one cooking apple (tart apple) per person. With a sharp knife, cut each apple through the skin only around the middle. Place the apples in an ovenproof dish and put a little water in the bottom. Fill the cavities with rum butter and a few raisins if wished. Bake in the centre of a preheated oven at 180°C, 350°F, Gas Mark 4 for about 30 minutes, basting occasionally with the juices.

Christmas Pies

Tuesday 29th December 1801
"We dined at the publick house on porridge with a second course of Christmas pies."

These pies were sometimes known as Cumberland Sweet Pies or Sweet Lamb Pies, and date back to the Middle Ages. Rum was often used, a commodity which the Wordsworths kept according to Dorothy for on 1st September 1800 she wrote, "We borrowed some bottles for bottling rum . . ."

Metric/Imperial	American
For the pastry:	For the pastry:
400 g/1 lb plain flour	2 cups all purpose flour
pinch of salt	pinch of salt
200 g/8 oz lard	1 cup shortening
4 x 15 ml spoons/4 tablespoons cold water	4–5 tablespoons cold water
For the filling:	For the filling:
200 g/8 oz raw lamb	½ lb raw lamb
150 g/6 oz currants	1 cup currants
150 g/6 oz raisins	1 cup raisins
100 g/4 oz soft brown sugar	½ cup soft brown sugar
4 x 15 ml/4 tablespoons rum or white wine	5 tablespoons rum or white wine
50g/2 oz candied peel	⅓ cup candied peel
1 x 2.5 ml spoon/½ teaspoon each of ground mace and nutmeg	½ teaspoon each of ground mace and nutmeg
salt and pepper	salt and pepper
butter	butter

Trim any fat from the meat and mince it. Put it in a pan with a little water and simmer until cooked. Drain and allow it to cool. Mix the meat with the other filling ingredients, except the butter.

Make the pastry by mixing the flour and salt together and rubbing in the fat until it resembles breadcrumbs. With a knife, stir the mixture with the cold water until it forms a stiff paste. Pull together and turn on to a floured board. Divide into two unequal pieces. Roll out the larger one and use it to line a deep pie dish. Moisten the edges with a little cold water. Add the pie filling and dot with butter. Roll out the rest of the pastry and form a lid, making a vent in the centre for the steam to escape. Seal the edges and decorate the top with pastry leaves. Brush with beaten egg and bake at 200°C, 400°F, Gas Mark 6 for about 40 minutes or until golden brown.

Brown Milk Coburg Loaf

Wednesday 2nd December 1801
"Mrs Olliff brought us some yeast . . ." and the next day, "We baked bread . . ." On 4th December "Mr Simpson and Charles Lloyd called for the yeast Receipt."

A 'Receipt' was an old word for recipe.

Flour was often adulterated in the nineteenth century, but the Wordsworths were once sent a "barrel of the best flour from America" by their good friend Mr Griffith. Dorothy baked some of this into small loaves which unfortunately were burned.

Dorothy baked bread two or three times a week when there were many mouths to feed, and on 5th December 1800 she wrote, "Sara and I had a grand bread and cake baking . . ." The fact that she mentioned the yeast specifically may have meant that it was unusual to use it — perhaps because it was scarce. This delicious recipe does not use yeast.

Metric/Imperial	American
225 g/8 oz wholemeal flour	2 cups Graham flour
225 g/8 oz plain flour	2 cups all purpose flour
1 x 5 ml spoon/1 teaspoon salt	1 teaspoon salt
1 x 5 ml spoon/1 teaspoon bicarbonate of soda	1 teaspoon baking soda
2 x 5 ml spoons/2 teaspoons cream of tartar	2 teaspoons cream of tartar
1 x 5 ml spoon/1 teaspoon sugar	1 teaspoon sugar
50 g/2 oz butter	½ stick butter
300 ml/½ pint milk	1¼ cups milk

Sift the flours and other dry ingredients together in a bowl and rub in the butter. Add the milk and mix well. Lift out the dough and knead lightly on a floured board. Shape into a neat round and place on a greased or non stick baking tray. With a sharp knife which has been dipped in flour, cut across the top of the dough to make a cross, and leave to rest for 5 minutes. Bake in a preheated oven at 190°C, 375°F, Gas Mark 5 for 30 minutes or until the loaf sounds hollow if tapped on the bottom. The loaf will have opened out into four corners:

Roast Hare

December 2nd 1800
. . . "*A pleasant moonlight evening, but not clear. Supped upon a hare. It came on a terrible evening. Hail, and wind, and cold, and rain.*"

One old recipe recommended that the hare be stuffed with forcemeat, spit roasted and basted continually with a pint of milk and then butter for an hour and a quarter. The following recipe requires less attention:

1 young hare which has been hung for a few days
a few slices of fat bacon
a large knob of cooking fat

For the stuffing:
175 g/6 oz/3 cups white breadcrumbs
100 g/4 oz/2 cups shredded suet
rind of half a lemon, grated
salt and pepper
a pinch of powdered mace
2 eggs
a little chopped parsley, sage, marjoram, thyme

First, make the stuffing by mixing the dry ingredients together well. Beat the eggs and add to the mixture which should then be firm and moist. Use this to fill the well cleaned body cavity of the hare and sew the sides together to retain the stuffing.

Lay the bacon slices over the back of the hare and place it in a roasting tin with the cooking fat. Roast for 1½–2 hours at 180°C, 350°F, Gas Mark 4, basting frequently to prevent dryness. Remove the bacon 15 minutes before the end of the cooking time to allow the hare to brown.

Serve with rich brown gravy made from the pan juices and red currant or rowan jelly.

Sweet Cake

Thursday 30th December 1802
Dorothy and William travelled to Keswick on horseback and on the way "stopped our horse close to the ledge opposite a tuft of primroses three flowers in full blossom and a Bud, they reared themselves up among the green moss." They ate some potted beef and sweetcake.

The old fashioned way of measuring cake ingredients was to weigh the eggs, then take that weight of flour, sugar and butter. This recipe is based on this formula.

Metric/Imperial	American
3 eggs (weighing 225 g/8 oz)	3 eggs (weighing ½ lb)
225 g/8 oz plain flour	2 cups all-purpose flour
2 x 5 ml spoons/2 teaspoons baking powder	2 teaspoons baking powder
225 g/8 oz caster sugar	1 cup superfine sugar
225 g/8 oz butter or margarine	2 sticks butter or margarine
grated rind of 1 lemon	grated rind of 1 lemon
a little milk	a little milk

Cream the butter and sugar with the lemon rind until light and fluffy. Sift the flour and baking powder together. Add one egg at a time to the butter mixture together with a tablespoon of flour, to prevent curdling. The eggs should be at room temperature. Fold in the remaining flour and mix with a little milk to a smooth dropping consistency. Bake at 160°C, 325°F, Gas Mark 3 for about 1 hour. Test with a skewer in the centre. If it comes out clean, the cake is done.

Potted Beef

Potted meats were traditionally prepared for travellers.

The remains of cold roast beef or boiled beef
100 g/4 oz/1 stick butter   a sprig of herbs
cayenne pepper to taste
2 large pinches of powdered mace

Remove all dry outside meat and gristle and mince the remainder. Add a little butter and the seasonings and mix well. Put it in a glass or earthen pot and lay a sprig of herbs on top e.g. parsley, thyme or marjoram and pour over clarified butter. This excludes the air and helps to preserve the meat.

JANUARY

·S·BASKERVILLE-MUSCUTT·

"We had ate up the cold turkey before we walked so we cooked no dinner. Sate a while by the fire and then drank tea at Frank Baty's. As we went past the Nab, . . I called. They gave me some nuts."

Honey Roast Turkey

Sunday 24th January 1802
"We went into the orchard as soon as breakfast was over laid out the situation for our new room, and sauntered a while. We had Mr Clarkson's turkey for dinner . . . After dinner I lay down till tea time."
and on 27th January,
"We ate up the cold turkey before we walked so we cooked no dinner."

Honey has been used since medieval times as a glaze. Despite its thickness it penetrates the skin leaving the meat tender and sweet while the skin is dark and shiny. The Wordsworths kept their own bees and would have had their own honey.

Metric/Imperial	American
1 medium sized turkey	1 medium sized turkey
100 g/4 oz honey	4 tablespoons honey
50 g/ 2 oz butter	½ stick butter
For the stuffing:	For the stuffing:
100 g/4 oz white breadcrumbs	2 cups white breadcrumbs
25 g/1 oz minced bacon	2 tablespoons minced bacon
2 medium sized cooking apples	2 medium sized tart apples
salt and pepper	salt and pepper
1 egg	1 egg
a little ham stock	a little ham stock
1 onion finely chopped	1 onion finely chopped
a little chopped parsley	a little chopped parsley

Prepare the marinade by melting the honey and butter together and when well mixed, pour it over the cleaned bird. Leave it in a cool place for 24 hours, spooning over the mixture occasionally.

To make the stuffing, mix the breadcrumbs, apple (peeled and finely chopped), bacon, onion, parsley, salt and pepper together. Add the beaten egg and enough stock to mix it to a firm consistency. Cook this separately in a tinfoil dish or use to stuff the bird and place it in a roasting tin. Cook for 20 minutes per pound (450 g), at 180°C, 350°F, Gas Mark 4, basting frequently with the honey mixture.

Westmorland Hams

1802 "On Saturday January 23rd we left Eusemere at 10 o'clock in the morning. I behind Wm Mr C on his Galloway. The morning not very promising the wind cold. The mountains large and dark but only thinly streaked with snow — a strong wind. We dined in Grisdale on ham bread and milk."

The Wordsworths had been staying with the Clarksons at Eusemere, Ullswater, and set off riding, Mr Clarkson on his Galloway pony.

Hams were cured in different ways all over England using wet pickles, dry salt or sweet cures, some with spices or herbs. Most hams were then smoked — but not the green Westmorland ham. This was laid for about four days in a special sweet cure of common salt, bay salt, saltpetre, black pepper and treacle. It would then be turned and rubbed twice a week for a month. *After soaking for twenty four hours in cold water, they were simply hung up to dry.*

The Wordsworths would probably have cured their own hams using a dry salt cure. The slate-topped table which can still be seen today in the Buttery which adjoins the kitchen at Dove Cottage was ideally suited for this since the brine needed to drain away. It would have dripped off the slate top on to the floor and seeped into the stream which runs beneath the floor tiles. The meat was placed on the slate top and salt was piled all over it. The salt needed to be changed frequently and a large bowl of fresh salt would probably have stood underneath the table. After a while the hams were rubbed with bran or sawdust to make a thin crust before being smoked. Smoking was often done in a recess in the chimney of the house, but if not, an inverted hogshead (barrel) was used.

To cook a smoked ham it first needed to be soaked in several changes of cold water. A pile of washed but unpeeled vegetables such as turnips, parsnips, carrots, celery and apples, together with a few fresh herbs — e.g. parsley, thyme, marjoram, etc. — were placed in the bottom of a large cooking pot with a few black peppercorns. The ham was laid on top and some sour cider and treacle (molasses) were poured over. Water to cover the joint was added and it was brought to the boil and simmered for about four hours. It was best to leave the ham to cool in the liquid and the skin was removed the next day. The fat was sprinkled with breadcrumbs and the joint held in front of the fire to 'blister' until brown and crisp. As the fat melted it held the crumbs and set them firmly when it cooled.

A mutton-ham was simply a leg of mutton cured in the same way.

Tapioca Pudding

On Tuesday 11th January 1803, it was a very cold day — too cold even for walking and after reading Chaucer's 'The Knight's Tale' Dorothy wrote, "Now I am going to take Tapioca for my supper; and Mary an Egg. William some cold mutton — his poor chest is tired."

Tapioca is unfashionable today; too many people perhaps having childhood memories of school dinners. It was recommended for the convalescent as it is easy to digest. It may be used in soups and broths or made into a pudding.

Metric/Imperial	American
75 g/3 oz tapioca	1/3 cup tapioca
1.2 litres/2 pints milk	5 cups (2 1/2 pints) milk
50 g/2 oz butter	1/2 stick butter
100 g/4 oz sugar	1/2 cup sugar
4 eggs	4 eggs
12 drops vanilla essence	12 drops vanilla extract
grated lemon rind	grated lemon rind
225 g/8 oz puff pastry	1/2 lb puff pastry

Wash the tapioca and stew it gently in the milk for 1/4 hour stirring occasionally. Allow to cool a little, mix in the butter, lemon rind, sugar, eggs (well beaten) and vanilla essence (extact). Butter a pie dish and line the edges with puff pastry. Put in the pudding and bake at 180°C, 350°F, Gas Mark 4 for one hour.

Filberts

The filbert is the cultivated hazel and the nuts were esteemed as a dessert. They were generally eaten with salt.

On Wednesday 27th January 1802 it was a beautiful mild morning — the sun shone, the lake was still, and all the shores reflected in it. After dinner Dorothy and William "Sate a while by the fire and then drank tea at Frank Baty's. As we went past the Nab, I was surprised to see the youngest child amongst the rest of them running about by itself with a canny round fat face, and rosy cheeks. I called in. They gave me some nuts — everybody surprised that we should come over Grisdale."

The Batys were close neighbours.

The nuts were probably filberts because on Wednesday 16th June 1802 Dorothy wrote,
"We walked towards Rydale for letters — met Frank Baty with the expected one from Mary. We went up into Rydale woods and read it there. We sate near an old wall which fenced a Hazel grove, which Wm said was exactly like the filbert grove at Middleham. It is a beautiful spot, a sloping or rather steep piece of ground, with hazels growing "tall and erect" in clumps at distances almost seeming regular as if they had been planted."

Filberts should always be served with the outer skin or husk on them, piled high on a dish with walnuts perhaps, with a fringe of leaves around the edge.

If you wish to store filberts, leave them on the tree until they are brown and ready to fall from their cups. They should be thoroughly dried on trays and then packed in containers with dry sand. First, put about a half inch (1 cm) of sand in the bottom of the chosen containers and cover with a layer of nuts. Sprinkle enough sand over them to cover and then a little cooking salt. Build up other layers in the same way until the container is full, finishing with a half inch (1 cm) layer of sand. Keep in a cool dry place, but not beyond March, otherwise the nuts begin to shrink.

Gingerbread

Sunday 16th January 1803
"Intensely cold. Wm had a fancy for some gingerbread. I put on Molly's cloak and my Spenser, and we walked towards Matthew Newton's. I went into the house. The blind Man and his wife and Sister were sitting by the fire, all dressed very clean in their Sunday's Clothes, the sister reading. They took their little stock of gingerbread out of the cupboard and I bought 6 pennyworth. They were so grateful when I paid them for it that I could not find it in my heart to tell them we were going to make Gingerbread ourselves. I had asked them if they had no thick. 'No', answered Matthew, 'There was none on Friday but we'll endeavour to get some.' The next Day the woman came just when we were baking and we bought 2 pennyworth."

Visitors to Grasmere will be familiar with Sarah Nelson's gingerbread which is sold from a small shop in the corner of the churchyard. The recipe is a closely guarded secret.

In 1819 the Grasmere rushbearers, by then almost solely children, were given gifts of 'Rushbearers' cake' — the. Grasmere gingerbread. This replaced an earlier custom whereby the rushbearers who undertook the strewing of the church floor — which was originally of soil — with fresh rushes were paid a fee which was usually spent on ale.

The 'thin' — as opposed to the thick — gingerbread is surprisingly hard. It is more like a thick biscuit. After a number of efforts, this is the most successful attempt:

Grasmere Gingerbread

Metric/Imperial	American
225 g/8 oz fine oatmeal	2 cups fine oatmeal
2 x 5 ml spoons/2 teaspoons ground ginger	2 teaspoons powdered ginger
100 g/2 oz glacé ginger finely minced	2 tablespoons glacé ginger finely minced
1 x 2.5 ml spoon/½ teaspoon bicarbonate of soda	½ teaspoon baking soda
1 x 2.5 ml spoon/½ teaspoon cream of tartar	½ teaspoon cream of tartar
1 tablespoon golden syrup	1 tablespoon light corn syrup
175 g/6 oz sugar	¾ cup sugar
50 g/2 oz butter	½ stick butter

Melt the syrup, sugar and butter together slowly in a pan. Meanwhile, mix the dry ingredients together and add the melted sugar mixture. Stir well until it forms a thick dryish paste. Grease a shallow baking tin and press the mixture in. It should be no more than one centimetre (5/16″) thick. Bake in a preheated oven at 170°C, 325°F, Gas Mark 3 for about 45 minutes. It should remain fairly pale in colour. Leave to cool in the tin but mark out into smallish squares before it cools completely.

Thick Gingerbread

This traditional recipe for thick gingerbread gives a dark cake. After cooking, leave it to mature for a few days before eating.

Metric/Imperial	American
225 g/8 oz treacle	⅔ cup molasses
225 g/8 oz golden syrup	⅔ cup light corn syrup
225 g/8 oz butter	2 sticks butter
225 g/8 oz brown sugar	1 cup brown sugar
25 g/1 oz ground ginger	2 tablespoons powdered ginger
450 g/1 lb plain flour	4 cups all-purpose flour
1 x 2.5 ml spoon/½ teaspoon powdered allspice	½ teaspoon powdered allspice
1 x 2.5 ml spoon/½ teaspoon bicarbonate of soda	½ teaspoon baking soda
150 ml/¼ pint warm milk	⅔ cup warm milk
3 eggs	3 eggs
pinch of salt	pinch of salt

Sift the flour and mix it with the sugar, ginger, allspice and salt. Melt the treacle, syrup and butter together and add to the dry ingredients, mixing well. Dissolve the bicarbonate of soda in the warm milk, whisk the eggs and mix both into the other ingredients. Mix well to form a smooth dough. Pour the mixture into a large square greased cake tin and bake at 180°C, 350°F, Gas Mark 4 for about an hour. To test if it is done, insert a skewer into the centre. If mixture sticks to it, it needs more cooking.

FEBRUARY

·S·BASKERVILLE-MUSCUTT·

"Before sunset I put on my shawl and walked out .. I stood at Sara's gate and when I came in view of Rydale I cast a long look upon the mountains beyond."

Roast Pork

Thursday 11th February 1802
. . . *"The Vale was bright and beautiful. Molly had linen hung out. We had pork to dinner sent us by Mrs Simpson."*

Whereas sage and onion stuffing and apple sauce are usually served with pork nowadays, in the early nineteenth century, it would probably have been served with pease pudding.

Metric/Imperial	American
1.75 kg/4 lb hand of pork	4 lb fresh picnic shoulder
olive oil	olive oil
salt	salt

If the skin is left on (as it is in England), score it to give a crisp crackling and rub with oil and salt. Put the joint in a preheated oven at 230°C, 450°F, Gas Mark 8, and turn it down to 180°C, 350°F, Gas Mark 4. Allow 30 minutes per 450 g/1 lb, plus 30 minutes.

Pease Pudding

This has traditionally been served with boiled or roast pork since the Middle Ages.

240 g/½ lb dried maincrop peas
sprigs of various herbs, e.g. parsley, mint, majoram and
    savoury
25 g/1 oz/1 tablespoon butter
salt and pepper
1 egg

Soak the peas overnight and in the morning, boil them until soft with the herbs. Take out the herbs, and drain the peas well. Rub them through a sieve or put them through a blender with the butter, salt and pepper and the beaten egg. Mix well. Fill a well greased pie dish with the mixture and bake in the oven for 30 minutes at 180°C, 350°F, Gas Mark 4.

Boiled Broccoli

Monday 9th June 1800
. . . *"In the evening I stuck peas, watered the garden and planted Brocoli . . ."*

This would have been ready for use in the early part of the following year.

Wash the broccoli well in cold water and drain. Strip off any coarse outer leaves, and remove the tough part of the stalk. Plunge it in boiling salted water for about 15 minutes or until tender but not too soft. Drain immediately and serve with lots of melted butter.

Stewed Pears

The Wordsworths had a pear tree in their garden at Dove Cottage, and may have stewed the pears this way.

Metric/Imperial	American
8 large pears	8 large pears
125 g/5 oz loaf sugar	½ cup loaf sugar
6 cloves	6 cloves
6 whole allspice	6 whole allspice
300 ml/½ pint water	1¼ cups water
150 ml/¼ pint port wine	⅔ cup port wine.
a few drops cochineal	a few drops red colouring

Peel the pears, halve them and remove the cores, leaving the stalks on. Put them in a pan with the other ingredients and let them simmer very gently until tender. Carefully lift them out on to a dish without breaking them. Boil up the syrup quickly for 2–3 minutes, allow it to cool and pour it over the pears and let them get perfectly cold.

German Carrots

On 16th May 1800 Dorothy helped Aggy Fisher a little to weed the carrots in the garden. Stored carefully the carrots would have lasted into the winter.

8 large carrots
75 g/3 oz/¾ stick butter
salt and pepper
grated nutmeg
1 x 15 ml spoon/1 tablespoon finely minced parsley
1 x 15 ml spoon/1 tablespoon minced onion
600 ml/1 pint/2½ cups weak stock
1 x 15 ml spoon/1 tablespoon flour

Wash, scrape and cut the carrots into rings 5 mm/¼″ thick. Melt most of the butter in a pan, toss the carrots with the salt, pepper, nutmeg, parsley and onion. Pour in the stock and simmer gently until almost tender. Drain and retain the liquid. In another pan, melt the rest of the butter, add the flour, and mix well until brown, slowly add the carrot liquid, let it boil and pour over the carrots. Finish simmering until tender.

Serve with roast pork.

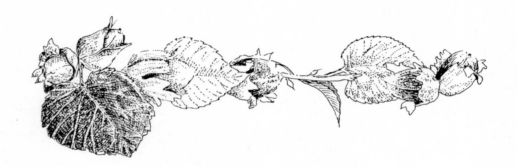

MARCH

"A fine pleasant day. We walked to Rydale . . The catkins are beautiful in the hedges. The ivy is very green."

Boiled Lamb with Onion Sauce

Lamb or mutton would have been the most widely available meat in Grasmere because of its then relatively remote situation.

Metric/Imperial	American
1 kg/2 lb shoulder of lamb	2 lb shoulder of lamb
a few whole black peppercorns	a few whole black peppercorns
1 x 5 ml spoon/1 teaspoon salt	a teaspoon salt
2 onions	2 onions
450 g/1 lb carrots	1 lb carrots
chopped mint or parsley	chopped mint or parsley
For the sauce:	For the sauce:
50 g/2 oz butter	½ stick butter
1 x 15 ml spoon/1 tablespoon plain flour	1 tablespoon all purpose flour
250 ml/½ pint milk	1¼ cups milk
125 ml/¼ pint lamb stock	⅔ cup lamb stock
2 large onions peeled and sliced thinly	2 large onions peeled and sliced thinly
salt and pepper	salt and pepper
a pinch of nutmeg	a pinch of powdered nutmeg

Chop the carrots and onions and place them in a large pan with the salt, peppercorns and the lamb. Add enough water to just cover the meat and bring to the boil. Boil for 20 minutes, remove from the heat and skim off the fat from the surface. Simmer for two hours, lift out and drain.

To make the onion sauce, soften the sliced onions in the butter over a gentle heat. Do not let them brown. Stir in the flour and cook for a few minutes. Slowly add the milk and stock mixing well. Bring to the boil stirring all the time and simmer for a few minutes until it thickens. Add the salt, pepper and nutmeg.

Pour the sauce over the sliced meat and serve garnished with chopped mint or parsley.

Seed Cake

Saturday Morning 13th March 1802
"It was as cold as ever it has been all winter very hard frost. I baked pies Bread, and seed-cake for Mr Simpson."

Seed cake was very popular from the sixteenth century to the end of the nineteenth century.

Metric/Imperial	American
225 g/8 oz self raising flour	2 cups self rising flour
pinch of salt	pinch of salt
100 g/4 oz butter	1 stick butter
100 g/4 oz sugar	½ cup sugar
25 g/1 oz caraway seeds	1 tablespoon caraway seeds
2 eggs	2 eggs
3 tablespoons milk	4 tablespoons milk

Mix the flour and salt in a basin. Rub in the fat with the fingertips until the mixture looks like breadcrumbs. Add the sugar and caraway seeds and mix well. Make a well in the centre and stir in the beaten eggs with just enough milk to mix to a smooth consistency. Beat well and pour into a greased and floured 20 cm/8 inch cake tin. Bake at 180°C, 350°F, Gas Mark 4 for 45 minutes or until a skewer inserted into the centre of the cake comes out clean.

Beefsteaks

On Wednesday 17th March 1802 Dorothy broiled beefsteaks, and the following day she wrote,
"A very fine morning. The sun shone but it was far colder than yesterday. I felt myself weak, and William charged me not to go to Mrs Lloyd's. I seemed indeed, to myself unfit for it but when he was gone I thought I would get the visit over if I could — So I ate a Beef-steak thinking it would strengthen me so it did, and I went off."

Dorothy would probably have used a gridiron to cook her steaks. This was a framework of parallel metal bars which was used to support meat or fish when it was grilled over a fire. Even in the nineteenth century they did not believe in overcooking a good steak. Mrs Beeton in her famous cookery book advocated that the steak be 1.5 cm/¾ inch thick or rather thinner. She levelled them by beating them as little as possible with a rolling pin and cooked them for only 8 or 10 minutes. To serve them she had ready a very hot dish, into which she had put a tablespoonful of mushroom ketchup, and a little minced shallot. They were rubbed over with butter and seasoned with salt and pepper before being dished up garnished with scraped horseradish or slices of cucumber.

Barley Broth

Sunday morning 14th March 1802:
"William had slept badly — he got up at 9 o'clock, but before he rose he had finished the Beggar Boys — and while we were at Breakfast that is (for I had breakfasted) he, with his Basin of Broth before him untouched and a little plate of Bread and butter he wrote the Poem to a Butterfly!"

William's broth was probably no more than a weak stock.

You probably won't like broth for breakfast — try this more substantial recipe for dinner instead!

Metric/Imperial	American
100 g/4 oz pearl barley	½ cup pearl barley
1 lt/2 pints mutton or beef stock	5 cups mutton or beef stock
150 ml/¼ pint milk	⅔ cup milk
a little chopped parsley	a little chopped parsley
1 onion	1 onion
1 carrot	1 carrot
1 small turnip	1 small turnip

Wash the carrot and turnip and peel the onion. Chop them all roughly. Simmer the barley in the stock with the vegetables for 2 hours. Remove the vegetables and skim the liquid. Add a little milk and chopped parsley to serve.

Honey Cakes

Using some of her honey instead of sugar, Dorothy could have produced these tasty cakes.

Metric/Imperial	American
300 g/12 oz self raising flour	1½ cups self rising flour
75 g/3 oz butter	¾ stick butter
1 egg	1 egg
2 x 15 ml spoons/2 tablespoons honey	3 tablespoons honey
milk	milk
1 x 5 ml spoon/1 teaspoon ground ginger	1 teaspoon ground ginger
1 x 5 ml spoon/1 teaspoon mixed spice	1 teaspoon mixed spice

Rub the butter into the flour; add the spice and ginger then the honey. Beat the egg with a little milk, then add to the other ingredients and mix well. Roll out the mixture on a floured board leaving it about 2.5 cm or an inch thick. Cut into small squares or rounds rather like scones. Bake on a floured tray at 220°C, 425°F, Gas Mark 7 for 20 minutes. Cool on a wire rack and eat freshly made.

Soda Cake

This old-fashioned cake is not often made today. It was cheap to make and probably would have appealed to Dorothy's sense of economy.

Metric/Imperial	American
450 g/1 lb plain flour	4 cups all purpose flour
225 g/8 oz sugar	2 cups sugar
225 g/8 oz currants	1½ cups currants
1 x 5 ml spoon/1 teaspoon bicarbonate of soda	1 teaspoon baking soda
2 eggs	2 eggs
225 g/8 oz margarine	1 cup margarine
grated lemon rind and nutmeg	grated lemon rind and nutmeg
pinch of salt	pinch of salt
150 ml/¼ pint boiling milk	⅔ cup boiling milk

Rub the fat into the flour, and mix well with the sugar. Add the boiling milk, stir well, then add the well-whisked eggs. Add the lemon rind, nutmeg and currants and beat well. Just before it is ready to put in the cake tin, add the soda and stir. Divide the mixture into the small greased cake tins and bake for 1 hour at 180°C, 350°F, Gas Mark 4.

APRIL

"I never saw daffodils so beautiful they grew among the mossy stones about and about them, some rested their heads upon these stones as on a pillow for weariness and the rest tossed and reeled and danced."

Blackcurrant Vinegar

Thursday 22nd April 1802
"Coleridge and I after dinner drank blackcurrants and water".

Dorothy would have preserved some of the previous year's crop of blackcurrants to serve them as a drink in April. This makes an excellent drink when diluted with cold water in summer, or with hot water in winter for coughs and sore throats.

Metric/Imperial	American
675 g/1½ lbs blackcurrants	1½ lbs blackcurrants
450 g/1 lb sugar per 600 ml/ pint of juice	2 cups sugar per 2½ cups of juice
600 ml/1 pint white wine vinegar	2½ cups white wine vinegar
1 wineglass brandy per 600 ml/ pint of juice (optional)	1 wineglass brandy per 2½ cups of juice (optional)

Wash the fruit and put it in a wide topped large jar with the vinegar. Cover and leave it to stand in a cool place for up to two weeks, shaking the jar each day. Drain off the liquid without pressing the fruit and strain. Add the sugar according to the amount of liquid and boil for about 10–15 minutes, removing any scum which forms. Add the brandy and when cold, bottle it and seal the jars well.

Minnow Tansies

Dorothy's brother John was a keen fisher in the lakes around Grasmere when he stayed at Dove Cottage. He and William often fished for pike. For bait they would have needed large minnows or small perch. Minnows, which are tiny fish found in shoals in the shallows of Cumbrian lakes, need not only be used as bait though as can be seen from this recipe by Izaak Walton from his book "The Compleat Angler" which was first published in 1653.

He says that in spring these little fish make "excellent Minnow-tansies; for being washed well in salt, and their heads and tails cut off, and their guts taken out, and not washed after, that is, being fried with yolks of eggs, the flowers of cowslips and of primroses, and a little tansy; thus used they make a dainty dish of meat."

If you wish to try this recipe take the following:

a few minnows
1 tablespoon of cowslips or primrose petals
2 egg yolks
100 g/4 oz/1 stick of butter
salt and pepper
tansy stalks

Crush the tansy stalks in a bowl to extract the juice, and remove the stalks. Add the egg yolks, petals, and seasoning and stir well. Coat the fish in the mixture and fry them, petals as well, in hot butter. Eat at once.

Rum Butter

There are many recipes for this very traditional lakeland delicacy. The Wordsworths bottled their own rum and, when they had a cow, made their own butter.
Originally it was the celebration fare on the birth of a baby, but it was also served with plain biscuits when visitors called.
Nowadays it is often eaten with scones, or Christmas pudding.

Metric/Imperial	American
225 g/8 oz unsalted butter	2 sticks unsalted butter
450 g/1 lb soft brown sugar	2 cups soft brown sugar
½ nutmeg, grated	½ nutmeg, grated
about 5 x 15 ml spoons/ 5 tablespoons rum	5 or 6 tablespoons rum

Soften the butter and beat in the sugar and nutmeg. Beat well and then gradually add the rum. Put into bowls and allow to set.

Havver Bread

Dorothy often baked bread which might have been this traditional Lakeland type. It is crispy rather like an oatcake. The name derives from the old Norse word "hafrar" meaning oats. It is delicious with cheese or jam, and with fish or meat pates.

Metric/Imperial	American
175 g/6 oz medium oatmeal	1 ½ cups medium oatmeal
50 g/2 oz brown flour	½ cup wholewheat flour
1 × 2.5 ml spoon/½ teaspoon salt	½ teaspoon salt
a pinch of bicarbonate of soda	a pinch of baking soda
1 × 15 ml spoon/1 tablespoon melted dripping	1 tablespoon melted shortening
boiling water	boiling water

Pour the melted dripping (shortening) on to the dry ingredients which have been mixed together. Mix with a little boiling water to make a dough. Turn it out on to a floured board and knead well. Roll it out quite thin. Cut into triangle shapes and cook for about 25 minutes at 180°C, 350°F, Gas Mark 4 until crisp and brown. Cool on a wire rack and store in an airtight box.

Baked Trout

Fish caught by William, and sometimes John when he stayed with them, helped to feed the household. Economical as ever, Dorothy "put up the bread with a few baked trouts."

An old nineteenth century recipe advocates baking the trout in buttered paper. A more modern version is to cook the trout in a parcel of foil.

1 trout per person (about 450 g/1 lb or less)
softened butter
sprigs of parsley and lemon thyme
lemon

Cut a piece of foil for each trout large enough to enclose it completely without bending the fish. Rub one side of the foil with butter. Clean and gut each fish. Place a knob of butter and a few herbs inside each fish. Dot with butter and place the fish on the buttered side of the foil. Wrap the foil round each fish and crimp the edges so that the juices do not escape. Place on a baking tray and cook for about 25 minutes at 200°C, 400°F, Gas mark 6. Serve the parcels directly on to the plates so that the aroma when opening the parcels can be enjoyed. Serve with lemon wedges.

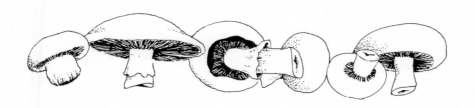

Bibliography

Book of Household Management by Mrs I Beeton (1861).

The Art of Cookery Made Plain and Easy by Hannah Glasse (1747).

The Universal Cookery Book (W. Foulsham & Co.)

The Compleat Angler by Izaak Walton (Dent – Everyman's Library)

The Good Wife's Cook Book (Jas Truscott & Son Ltd.)

Lakeland Recipes Old and New by Jean Poulson (Countryside Publications)

Life and Tradition in the Lake District by William Rollinson (Dalesman, 1981)

Letters of Dorothy Wordsworth: A selection edited by Alan G. Hill (Oxford University Press, 1981)

Journals of Dorothy Wordsworth, 2nd edition edited by Mary Moorman (Oxford University Press, 1981)

Index